D0816520

HOW THINGS HAVE CHANGED

Vacations
and Holidays

Jon Richards

Chrysalis Education

This U.S. edition copyright © 2005 Chrysalis Education
Published in conjunction with Chrysalis Books Group Plc

International copyright reserved in all countries.
No part of this book may be reproduced in any
form without written permission from the publisher.

Distributed in the United States by
Smart Apple Media
2140 Howard Drive West
North Mankato, Minnesota 56003

Library of Congress Control Number: 20041108647

ISBN 1-59389-197-0

A Cataloging-in-Publication record for this book is
available from the Library of Congress.

Editorial Manager: Joyce Bentley
Editorial Assistant: Camilla Lloyd
Produced by Tall Tree Ltd.
Designer: Ed Simkins
Editor: Kate Simkins
Consultant: Jon Kirkwood
Picture Researcher: Lorna Ainger

Printed in China

Some of the more unfamiliar words used in this book
are explained in the glossary on page 31.

Contents

Festival days

Holidays began as special days to celebrate religious festivals—the word "holiday" comes from the phrase "holy day." Today, a holiday is a period of time that people take off from work or school to rest, travel, or have fun.

People in Ancient Egypt were allowed 70 days off each year for religious festivals, while the Romans had more than 100 holidays to celebrate their gods. Pilgrimages, in which a person traveled to a holy site to worship, were another form of religious break. Many pilgrimages are still undertaken today. One of these is the *Hajj*, the Muslim pilgrimage to Mecca in Saudi Arabia.

◀ *This medieval carving shows people on a Christian pilgrimage. Popular Christian destinations include Rome and Jerusalem.*

◀ In 17th-century Germany, people started to bring trees into their houses and decorate them for the Christmas holidays.

As important events occurred, people took time off to celebrate them and the people these were associated with. Martin Luther King Day in the US is a popular example, as is Republic Day in India, which commemorates the start of the Indian Republic in 1950.

LOOK CLOSER

Kumbh Mela is a Hindu pilgrimage to rivers in India. Pilgrims bathe in the rivers to clean their bodies and souls. Some 20 million people make this pilgrimage every year, making it the largest religious gathering in the world.

Long breaks

The first long vacations were taken by wealthy Romans, who went to their villas to escape the city in the hot summer. Improved travel has allowed more people to take long breaks and to experience different cultures.

Many Roman villas were built around pools of water, which would help to keep the houses cool in summer. This was in contrast to the densely packed streets of the cities, that would be unbearably hot at this time.

▶ This painting shows a Roman villa. The Emperor Hadrian (AD 117–138) had a villa in Tivoli, Italy, that was surrounded by exotic gardens.

6

LOOK CLOSER

From the mid-16th century, young, rich men from England were sent around Europe in the company of a tutor to improve their education. This vacation became known as the Grand Tour. Popular cities on the tour were Paris and Rome. In this painting, tourists are visiting the Pantheon in Rome.

Due to the development of cheap travel today, far more people are able to visit other countries. One popular form of the long vacation is "backpacking," which is an inexpensive break where people travel with backpacks and stay in budget hostels around the world.

◀ Many young people go backpacking in the "gap year" between school and university.

7

Short breaks

Some vacations may last just a few days or two to three weeks. These short breaks were not affordable to all at first, but they soon became popular, helped by the introduction of a new kind of vacation—the package tour.

The South Metropolitan Gas Company of Britain was one of the first companies to give its workers paid vacations, in 1871. Paid vacations enabled families to afford short breaks. Initially, these were taken in resorts that were near to home, since travel was still expensive.

▼ Beach vacations are a favorite destination for a short break. People are attracted by the good weather and the experience of visiting a different part of the country or even a foreign country.

8

The introduction of package tours and the reduction in the cost of travel after World War II (1939–45) created a boom in vacations in foreign countries. Today, for example, more than 75 million people travel to France every year, making it the world's most popular tourist destination.

▲ For Europeans, weekend breaks to cities such as Venice have been made more popular in recent years due to the availability of cheap flights.

EUREKA!

In 1841, Thomas Cook organized a day trip from Leicester to Loughborough, UK, and established the world's first travel agency. When he died in 1892, the Thomas Cook agency was the largest in the world.

9

Places to stay

People need a place to stay when they go away. The first accommodation for travelers were inns along a road. Later came luxury hotels, boarding houses, and motels.

The Ancient Persians, whose empire flourished over 2,500 years ago, built small inns along their roads called *caravanserais*; and the Romans had small hotels called *mansionis*. In the Middle Ages, travelers could stay in monasteries along the way.

▼ *Traveling by coach in the 18th century took a long time. Coach houses were set up along routes so that people could rest, eat, and sleep, and the horses could be changed.*

10

EUREKA!

American Kemmons Wilson revolutionized the hotel industry when he opened his first Holiday Inn in Memphis in 1952. Wilson's idea was to offer travelers a reliable standard of affordable accommodation. Previously, hotels varied greatly in standards and price. Within 25 years, there were 1,700 Holiday Inns around the world.

Train travel arrived in the 19th century, and with it came the first large-scale hotels. Today, giant hotels are built to cater to huge numbers of tourists. The world's largest is the MGM Grand in Las Vegas, with 5,005 rooms.

◀ Hotels began to use a system of stars in the 1830s to represent quality. A luxury hotel, such as the Ritz in London, England, shown here, will have five stars.

11

Under canvas

Summer camps range from a simple campsite where people can pitch a tent to enormous family resorts that are equipped with every kind of facility a family could need on vacation.

The first children's summer camps were started in the US in around 1885. They were designed to give children from the city a taste of country life. At first, they were only for boys. The first camps for girls started to appear at the end of the 19th century.

◀ Kids' camps offer several weeks of activities throughout the school summer vacation.

LOOK CLOSER

Camping has long been popular for vacations because tents offer a cheap and easy form of accommodation—all you need is a campsite to stay in. Modern tents make it even easier, since some models are designed to "pop" open using a spring-loaded frame.

The first specially built vacation camp for adults was set up on the Isle of Man, UK, in 1894. It was just for men and offered very basic facilities. In contrast, modern campsites can be found worldwide and offer a variety of facilities. Some even cater to specialized activities, such as tennis and horseback riding.

▼ Modern family camps have restaurants, swimming pools, and entertainment facilities. Some cover more than 485 acres (160 hectares)—that's about the size of 230 football fields.

13

Resorts

The 19th century saw the expansion of vacation resorts–specially designed places that cater to the needs of vacationers. Today, there are beach resorts, as well as health spas and sports resorts.

The earliest resorts were designed to improve a person's health. The spa waters in Bath, England, were first used for their healing powers in 836 BC. During the 18th century, coastal towns became popular after doctors commented on the health benefits of seawater.

▼ Today, many people prefer to visit beach resorts in foreign countries. In 2002, over 23 million US residents traveled to foreign countries.

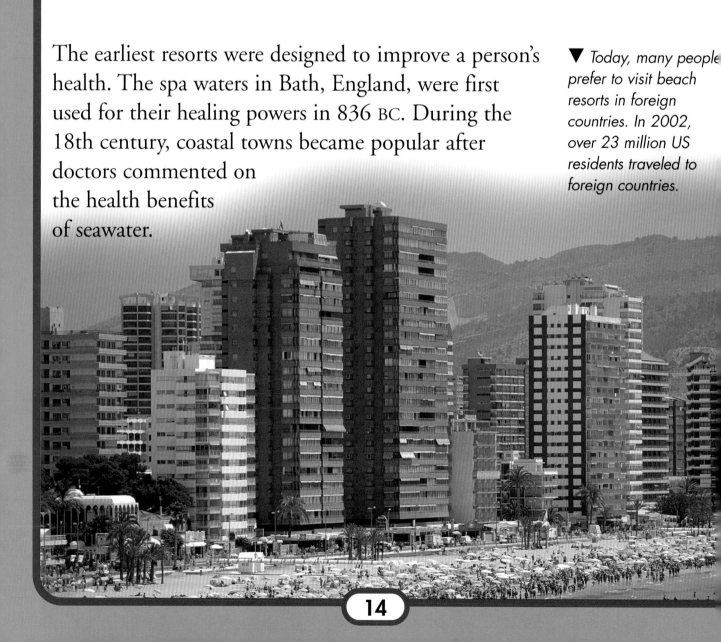

14

◀ *Ski resorts offer accommodation, restaurants, bars, and access to ski slopes via lifts and cable cars. The first cable car for skiers opened at the Swiss resort of Klosters in 1932.*

As tourist numbers increased, so did the amount of money generated by tourism, and vacation resorts became an important part of every country's income. Today, the tourist industry creates some 476 billion dollars' worth of income worldwide each year.

LOOK CLOSER

Safaris are vacations where tourists can see wildlife in its natural setting. Safari lodges are built in national parks and nature reserves so that the tourists are near the animals. Specially trained guides advise and take care of the tourists.

Boats and cruising

Traveling by boat used to be the quickest method of going to distant countries. Today, it has become a popular way to spend a vacation, with people cruising in vast ocean liners, sailing in yachts, or traveling along rivers in small boats.

When the steamship *Great Western* crossed the Atlantic Ocean in 1838, it took just 15 days, halving the time taken by sailing ships. After World War I (1914–18), the conversion of many warships into large passenger ships called liners helped to reduce the cost of cruising and make it more popular.

▼ By the 1920s, when this photo was taken, cruise liners could carry nearly 2,500 people.

16

In recent years, the variety of boat
vacations has increased. Large
liners still cruise the oceans, while
many tour operators now run
sailing trips, where people can
learn how to sail a yacht.

▲ *Canal narrow boats, which once pulled
cargo, have been converted into boats for
cruising canals and rivers.*

LOOK CLOSER

Modern ocean liners are
equipped with the most
luxurious facilities. The *Queen
Mary II* can carry 2,620
passengers. Some of the rooms inside are
equipped with their own private elevator,
two bathrooms, and a balcony. There are
also ten restaurants to choose from.

17

Train travel

From the mid-19th century, regular train services gave vacationers easy access to resorts at home and abroad, and train travel was available to both the rich and less wealthy. Modern trains still carry tourists on vacation, but at much greater speeds.

The expansion of railroad networks in the last half of the 19th century linked large cities with resorts, while crossing entire continents. Local day trips became possible, and long, luxurious journeys by rail were soon popular with the rich.

▼ The Orient Express train ran from Paris to Constantinople (now Istanbul). It started in 1883 and passengers traveled in luxury.

18

The railroad across the USA opened in 1869 and was the world's first transcontinental railroad. Tourists can still travel this route in trains pulled by steam locomotives.

Competition from the plane and the car in the last half of the 20th century saw a decline in the use of train travel. Even so, trains are still a popular method of travel and fast diesel and electric trains, such as the French TGV, carry thousands of tourists to destinations at more than 185 mph (300 km/h).

EUREKA!

The earliest sleeper cars were introduced on US trains in 1836, but passengers had to bring their own bedding. The first rail carriage that was specifically designed for comfortable nighttime travel was created by George Pullman and Ben Field, nearly 30 years later, in 1865.

The open road

The increase in affordable cars changed how people traveled on vacation. New roads were built to carry the greater number of drivers, and vehicles were developed that allowed tourists to take their accommodation with them.

In 1909, Henry Ford introduced the world's first affordable car, the Model T. Suddenly, cars were available to millions of people, and many started to drive them to travel on vacation. Cars were used to pull campers, and trucks were converted to create mobile homes.

▼ These travelers from the 1920s are eating their meal on the side of the road since there were few roadside facilities available to the driver.

Today, the car is an essential part of vacationing. About 80 percent of all trips are made by car, and vacation resorts take this into account. For example, Disneyland's California Adventure resort, which opened in 2001, was built with a parking lot big enough to hold 10,242 cars.

▲ *This camper can sleep six people, with two people sleeping in the space above the driver's cab.*

LOOK CLOSER

Campers and mobile homes are equipped with all the appliances of a modern home. These include a full kitchen and washroom. The power to run all of these appliances comes from batteries or from electrical supply points at a campsite.

21

Air travel

The airplane revolutionized travel after the creation of the first airlines in 1919. Since then, it has allowed tourists to visit places that would have been difficult to reach in the past.

The first airlines used old military aircraft. Passengers had to wear thick clothes to stay warm and cotton in their ears to block out the engine noise. By the mid-1920s, standards had improved, and airlines offered in-flight food and movies.

▼ Seaplanes and flying boats were used for flights from the 1920s. They could fly long distances in short hops from port to port.

22

The first jet airliner was the de Haviland Comet, introduced in 1952. Jet airliners could fly farther and faster than propeller aircraft. As a result, air travel became cheaper and available to more people, allowing them to visit and experience foreign places and cultures.

▲ Also called the Jumbo Jet, the Boeing 747 can carry more than 500 people and travel for over 8,400 miles (13,500 km) without refueling.

LOOK CLOSER

Modern airports are enormous. The busiest is Hartsfield International Airport in Atlanta, which serves over 80 million people every year, as well as handling their baggage. It has huge areas for runways and air-traffic control.

23

Traveling light

The travel industry has created a huge demand for a wide range of products and accessories to help the traveler. These include strong and light luggage, miniaturized electric devices, and vaccinations to prevent disease.

As long ago as the 17th century, travelers were aware that certain substances could protect them from illness. Quinine, made from the bark of a tree, was noted for curing malaria in 1633. Today, there are vaccinations for a wide range of diseases, as well as chemical insect repellents and suntan creams.

▼ Early luggage consisted of wooden crates, leather cases, and simple sacks. Modern luggage is made from artificial materials that are strong and light.

24

◀ *This travel iron is just 7.5 in (19 cm) long and weighs only 1.5 lb (0.7 kg). Other miniaturized electric travel accessories include hair driers and alarm clocks.*

Many modern accessories are designed to be small and light to save space. Clothing that is specially designed for travelers is made from materials that are lightweight, easy to pack, and quick drying.

EUREKA!

The first suntan cream appeared in 1936. It was called Ambre Solaire and was made by L'Oreal. Suntan creams protect against harmful rays from the sun and are available as creams, oils, sprays, lotions, or foam.

Paperwork

People can move freely around their country of birth, but they need official documents called passports in order to enter another country. These have photographs and information that identify the traveler.

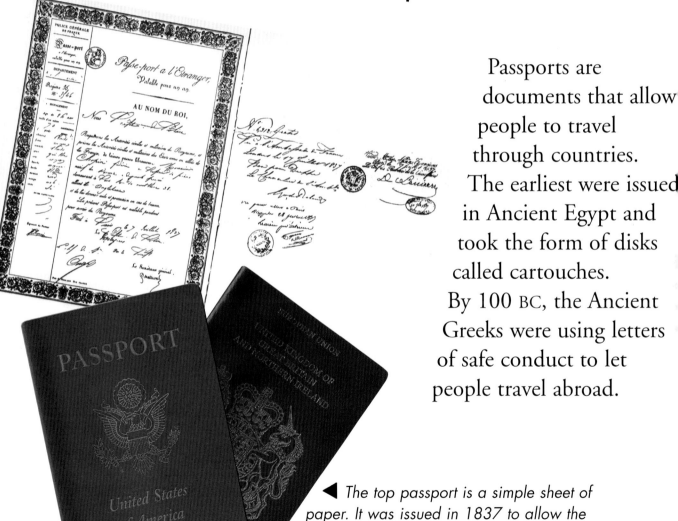

Passports are documents that allow people to travel through countries. The earliest were issued in Ancient Egypt and took the form of disks called cartouches. By 100 BC, the Ancient Greeks were using letters of safe conduct to let people travel abroad.

◀ The top passport is a simple sheet of paper. It was issued in 1837 to allow the Polish composer Chopin to visit Great Britain. In 1916, booklet passports, similar to those used today, were introduced.

In addition to a passport, many countries require travelers to apply for visas. These are documents that give permission to enter a country on a specific trip and for a set period of time. Threats to national security have also seen some countries demanding that passports are equipped with a computer chip. This will store unique identifying details about the traveler, such as fingerprints.

▲ *Publishers produce travel guides to help people find their way around. They became popular after German, Karl Baedeker, published his first guide in 1829.*

EUREKA!

In 1891, the American Express company introduced traveler's checks. These allowed people to take out local currency while abroad. This reduced the amount of cash and foreign currency that people had to carry around with them.

27

Timeline

• 1836. The first railroad sleeper cars are introduced in the US.

• c.836 BC. The hot springs in Bath, England, is visited for its healing powers.

• c.1550. Young, wealthy men start touring the cities of Europe in what became known as the Grand Tour.

• 1841. Thomas Cook starts to organize trips and sets up the world's first travel agency.

• 1633. Quinine is first used for its ability to cure malaria.

• 1865. George Pullman and Ben Field design the first specially built railroad sleeper cars

900 BC

• c.1830. A star system is adopted to grade the quality of hotels.

• 1869. The world's first transcontinental railroad opens the US.

• 1829. Karl Baedeker publishes his first travel guide.

• AD 117–138. Roman Emperor Hadrian builds a villa in Tivoli, Italy.

• c.100 BC. The Ancient Greeks start to use letters of safe conduct as early passports.

28

• 1871. The South Metropolitan Gas Company gives its workers paid vacations.

• 1883. The first Orient Express train runs between Paris and Constantinople.

• c.1885. The first summer camps for children are started in the US.

• 1894. The first specially built camp for adults is opened on the Isle of Man, UK.

• 1932. The world's first cable car for skiers opens in Klosters, Switzerland.

• 1936. Ambre Solaire makes the world's first suntan cream.

• 1970. Boeing 747 Jumbo Jet enters service.

• 2004. Passports are introduced containing computer chips with information about the passport owner.

TODAY

• 1919. The first airlines are formed.

• 1916. Booklet passports are introduced.

• 1909. Henry Ford introduces the Model T, the world's first affordable car.

• 1952. The de Haviland Comet becomes the world's first jet-powered airliner.

• 1952. Kemmons Wilson opens the first Holiday Inn hotel.

• 1891. American Express releases the first traveler's checks.

29

Factfile

• The English word "posh" comes from a term used to describe a type of ticket bought for people traveling between Great Britain and India in the 19th century. Wealthy travelers wanted the most comfortable cabins, and these were on the shaded side of the ship. On the journey out, these cabins were on the port side, and on the starboard side for the journey back. People wanting these cabins would ask for a "posh" ticket: Port Out, Starboard Home.

• The fastest jet airliner was the Tupolev Tu-144 from the Soviet Union. It could fly at 1,600 mph (2,587 km/h)—that's two-and-a-half times the speed of sound!

• The US has more airports than any other country, with 14,459. The next country is Brazil, which has 3,291.

• The world's oldest hotel is the 100-room Hoshi Ryokan in Awazu, Japan. It dates back to AD 717 and was built near a hot spring, that people visited for its healing powers.

• The world's busiest international air route is between Taipei in Taiwan and Hong Kong in China. Every year, nearly four million people fly this route. The second-busiest international route is between London in the UK and Dublin in the Republic of Ireland.

Glossary

Backpacking
Traveling around without staying in one place for too long. It gets its name from the backpacks that people carry with them and use to store their clothes and possessions.

Currency
The money used in a particular country.

Motel
A roadside hotel that is designed to cater to motorists.

Narrow boat
A thin barge that was used to carry industrial cargo along canals. Today, many of these boats have been converted into homes and pleasure boats.

Package tour
A vacation where everything is arranged by a travel agent. This includes travel, accommodation, and sometimes meals.

Passport
An official document or booklet that identifies a traveler and allows them to travel from one country to another.

Persian
A person from the ancient civilization that flourished around 2,500 years ago in the Middle East.

Pilgrimage
A journey that is made to a holy site for religious reasons.

Quinine
A chemical taken from the bark of the cinchona tree. Quinine has been used to fight the effects of the disease malaria.

Republic
A country in which the elected government is the highest power.

Travel agency
An organization that arranges vacations for people.

Vaccination
A type of medicine, often injected, that protects a person against a certain disease.

Villa
A large house in the country. Roman villas were usually built around a pool of water, and indeed, today, many vacation villas have pools.

Index